MORE

OF THE
WORLD'S
STUPIDEST
SIGNS

Since the publication of our previous silly signs collections, *Please Take Advantage of the Chambermaid* and *The World's Stupidest Signs*, eagle-eyed readers have been sending in scores of sightings. A very big thank you to everyone who contributed! If you would like to send in stupid signs for our next book, please email them to:

jokes@michaelomarabooks.com

MORE

of THE
WORLD'S STUPIDEST SIGNS

Michael O'Mara Humour

First published in Great Britain in 2003 by
Michael O'Mara Books Limited
9 Lion Yard
Tremadoc Road
London SW4 7NQ

A CIP catalogue record for this book is available from the
British Library

ISBN 1-84317-032-9

7 9 10 8

Edited by Bryony Evens

Designed and typeset by Design 23

www.mombooks.com

Printed and bound in Britain
by Cox and Wyman Ltd, Reading, Berks

Whole Chicken Medium Fresh

From a supermarket leaflet in South London

Please do not lock the door as we have lost the key.

In an Irish hotel room

Valour Waistcoats

In the Covent Garden branch of a clothing chain

Mental Health Prevention Center

In a New York medical building

Barefoot customers will not be entertained

**In the cinema at Rotorua,
New Zealand**

Archery Tournament

Ears Pierced

Adjacent signs outside a
shopping mall

We will sell gasoline to anyone in a glass container

At an American gas station

KEEP

DOOR

CLOSE

●●●●●●●●●●●●

WARNING
Footpath Unsuitable for Pedestrians

Twenty-two members were present at the church meeting held at the home of Mrs Marsha Crutchfield last evening. Mrs Crutchfield and Mrs Rankin sang a duet, 'The Lord Knows Why'.

During the
absence of our
vicar, we enjoyed
the rare privilege
of hearing a
good sermon when
J. F. Stubbs
supplied our
pulpit.

Ushers
will eat
latecomers.

The third verse
of 'Blessed
Assurance'
should be sung
without musical
accomplishment.

The audience
is asked to
remain
seated until
the end of
the recession.

The choir
invites any
member of the
congregation
who enjoys
sinning to
join the
choir.

The Pastor
would appreciate
it if the
ladies of the
congregation
would lend him
their electric
girdles for the
pancake breakfast
next Sunday
morning.

The vicar
will preach his
farewell message,
after which the
choir will sing
'Break Forth
Into Joy'.

The Reverend
Merriweather
spoke briefly,
much to the
delight of the
audience.

Leather Faced Ladies Handbags

On a market stall

NO MUDDY BOOTS PLEASE OR DOGS SMOKING ICE CREAMS

Sign on the door of a souvenir shop in Porlock Weir, Somerset

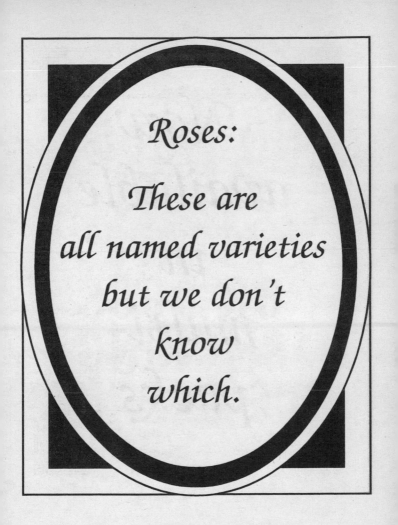

Roses:

These are
all named varieties
but we don't
know
which.

At a garden centre

Now available in multi-packs

**On a display of 'I Love You Only'
Valentine cards**

Don't let your worries kill you. Let the church help.

CAUTION:
Do not run on the stairs. Use the handrail.

Sign at a rail station

One can peel tomatoes easily by standing in boiling water for a minute.

In the cookery column of
the *Daily Mail*

Anyone caught hanging from the rim will be suspended

At a basketball court

No Cycling Dogs On Leads

Bridge out
Open to local traffic

When this sign is under water, this road is impassable

On a Tennessee highway

It is forbidden to drop hitchhikers on the motorway

On a bridge over the M4 motorway in Berkshire, England

Drive In Car Park

This Sign Not In Use

On a motorway north of
London, England

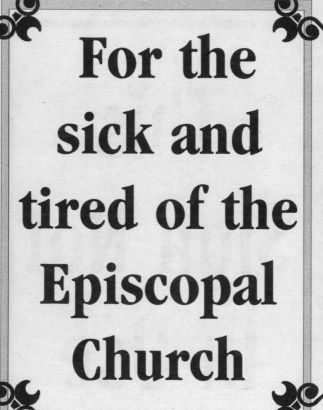

For the sick and tired of the Episcopal Church

On a New York convalescent home

(AMUSEMENTS→) (Toilets)

**Signs in Bournemouth,
Dorset, England**

Big
Dick's
Halfway
Inn

At a resort in the USA

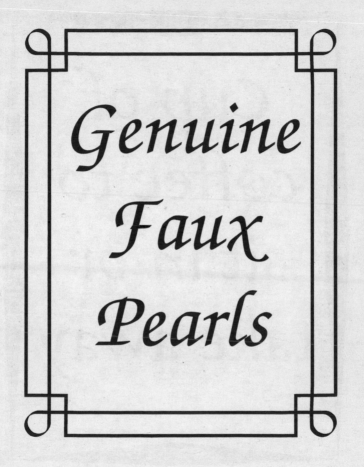

Genuine Faux Pearls

In a jewellery store

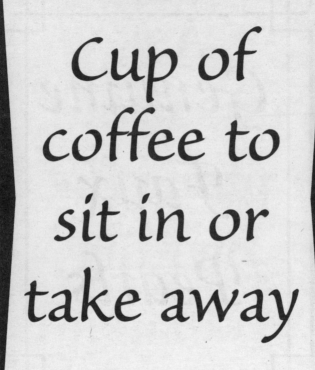

Cup of coffee to sit in or take away

**Outside a coffee shop in Malvern,
Worcestershire, England**

Ask about our plans for owning your home

In the offices of a loan company

GBH

Fitness

Club

Sign in Stratford-upon-Avon, England

In the interest of safety, it is advisable to keep your child away from fire & flames

Label on a cot blanket and children's clothing from a famous British high-street store

Do not pour liquids into your television set

USER INSTRUCTIONS:
Remove outer packaging. Wash with soap in warm water to form lather.

Rinse off and dry.

On a supermarket own-brand
bar of soap

WARNING!
When motor is running the blade is turning

On a lawnmower

100% pure all-natural fresh-squeezed orange juice from concentrate

On a carton of orange juice

WARNING: Contents flammable

On a container of lighter fluid

CAUTION: Contents may catch fire

On a box of matches

Not to be used as a hairdryer

On a paint-stripper gun

Do not swim
beyond the buoys.
No one in the town is
expected to save you
if you fail to heed
this warning.

Sign in a village on the Black Sea

Restricted to unauthorized personnel

At a number of British military bases

Monster

Man

Eating

Shark

At a zoo

Bottomless Pit
65 feet deep

NOW IS THE SUMMER OF OUR DISCOUNT TENTS

In the window of a camping shop
in Bolton, Lancashire, England

Able to do the worst possible job

Sign in a drycleaner's

Does your child wet the bed? Enquire within.

Sign outside a chemist's shop in Liverpool in the 1960s

GOD IS GOOD.
Dr Hargreaves
is better.

On a church notice board during the minister's illness

Scouts
are saving
aluminium cans,
bottles, and
other items to
be recycled.
Proceeds will
be used to
cripple
children.

Due to the
Rector's
illness,
Wednesday's
healing
services
will be
discontinued
until further
notice.

Hymn 43:
'Great God,
What Do I See
Here?'

Preacher:
The Reverend
Horace Blodgett

Hymn 47:
'Hark! An Awful
Voice Is Sounding'

Today's
Sermon:
'How Much Can
A Man Drink?'
with hymns
from
a full
choir.

The older children will be presenting Shakespeare's *Hamlet* in the church basement on Friday at 7pm. The congregation is invited to attend this tragedy.

Please join
us as we show
our support
for Amy and
Alan in
preparing for
the girth of
their first
child.

The music
for today's
service was
composed by
George
Friedrich
Handel in
celebration
of the 300th
anniversary
of his birth.

Will the last person to leave please see that the perpetual light is extinguished.

In the vestry of a church in the USA

In case of fire, please pay bill promptly

In a café in Cambridge

Be careful! Goats like to nibble at your clothes and butt

At a petting zoo

NOTICE – PUBLIC BAR

Our public bar is presently not open because it is closed

Manager

Outside a bar in Africa

Broken lenses duplicated here

In an optician's

fifteen men's wool suits, £50. They won't last an hour.

In a gentleman's outfitters

DANGER
PLEASE
KEEP
OUT

• • • • • • • • •

Sign seen on a litter bin

PLEASE DO NOT SPIT TOO LOUD. THANK YOU.

Malaysian street sign

Don't kill your wife, let us do it!

Outside a launderette in East London

DANGER CHILDREN KEEP OUT

Seen on a wire-mesh fence surrounding a building site

In event of air attack drive off bridge

On the Triborough Bridge in New York

Toilet →

Stay in your car

Parking for Drive-Thru Service Only

At a burger bar in the USA

Caution Tree in Centre of Road

No Parking Above This Sign

Danger Ahead Fasten Safety Belts And Remove Dentures

Sign near a river in Europe

Animals Drive Very Slowly

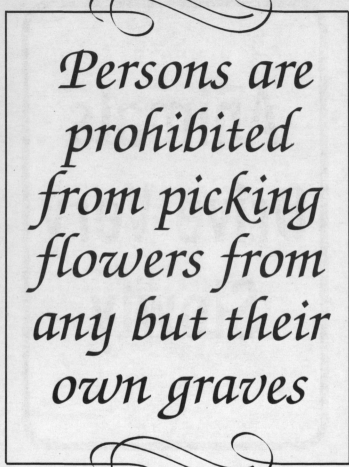

Persons are prohibited from picking flowers from any but their own graves

In a Pennsylvania cemetery

Sheep,
please
keep dogs
under
control

Sign on farmland in England

. . . died after a long fight with his family in Cheltenham

Please do not touch this exhibit

Braille sign at a museum in London

PLANTS
PRODUCE
FLOWERS

**In a country lane near Horsham,
West Sussex**

Open
seven days
a week
and
weekends

In a restaurant

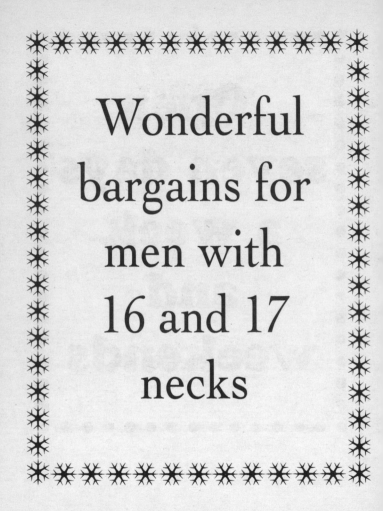

Wonderful bargains for men with 16 and 17 necks

In a clothing store

MAYDAY
Please do not smash our windows.

Macdonalds →
← Starbucks

For directions, please ask inside

Sign on a café in London during the
Mayday anti-capitalist rally, 2001

Tourist Information & Travel Services (T.I.T.S.)

Sign in Nepal

Eight new choir robes are currently needed, due to the addition of several new members and to the deterioration of some older ones.

Evening
massage –
6pm.

This evening at 7pm there will be a hymn sing in the park opposite the church. Bring a blanket and come prepared to sin.

The concert was a great success. Special thanks are due to the minister's daughter, who laboured the whole evening at the piano, which as usual fell upon her.

Next Sunday
Mrs Vinson
will be
soloist for
the morning
service. The
vicar will
then speak on
'It's a
Terrible
Experience'.

The outreach committee has enlisted 25 visitors to make calls on people who are not afflicted with any church.

A song
fest was
hell at the
Methodist
Church on
Wednesday.

Outside a petrol station in Africa

We Specialize in Quick Erections

Outside a construction company
in England

TRESPASERS WILL BE SHOT. SURVIVERS WILL BE SHOT AGAIN.

On farmland

All persons (except players) caught collecting balls on this course will be prosecuted and have their balls removed.

At a golf course

Those who throw objects at the crocodiles will be asked to retrieve them.

At a zoo

Master Baiter

At a fishing-tackle store in the USA

38 years on the same spot

●●●●●●●●●●

**On a long-established
New Mexico drycleaner's**

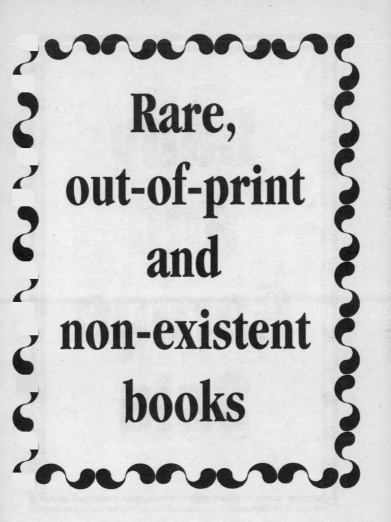

Rare, out-of-print and non-existent books

In an American bookstore

Baby
and
Garage
Sale

Safe for carpets, too!

On a tin of carpet cleaner

No keyboard detected. Press any key to continue.

Computer error message

Remove before driving

On a car windscreen frost cover

Do not put wet clothes in dryers, as this can cause irreparable damage.

In a launderette

DO NOT ACTIVATE WITH WET HANDS

Sign on a hand-dryer in a public toilet

IF BUILDING IN WHICH HEATER RESIDES IS ON FIRE, DO NOT GO INTO BUILDING.

On a gas water heater

This floodlight is capable of illuminating large areas, even in the dark.

On a floodlight

Planned Parenthood

-IN THE REAR→

Outside a family-planning clinic in the USA

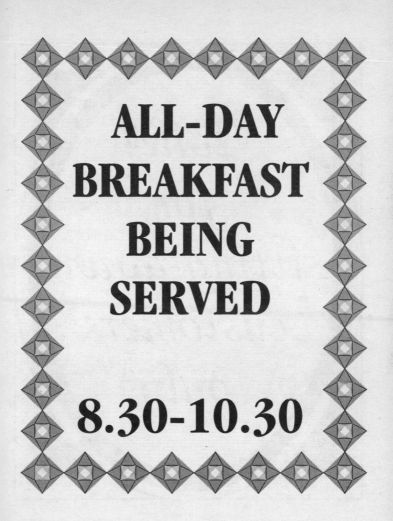

**ALL-DAY
BREAKFAST
BEING
SERVED**

8.30-10.30

In a café

Toilet for sitting-down customers only

In a Scottish teashop

Fine for Littering

On a California freeway

CARTER,
WHEY
&
TIPPETT

Rubbish-removal firm in London

Frozen
Supervisor

Position advertised in a supermarket

Craft shop left under bridge

Sign in London

Sid's
Pants
is
Open

**In the window of an Atlanta
clothing store**

During vacation of owner, a competent hair stylist will be here

In a barbershop

Eat What You Like Only £9.95

Children Only £2.95

In a buffet restaurant

Michael O'Mara Humour

All Michael O'Mara titles are available by post from:
Bookpost, PO Box 29, Douglas, Isle of Man, IM99 1BQ

Credit cards accepted. Telephone: 01624 677237 Fax: 01624 670923
Email: bookshop@enterprise.net Internet: www.bookpost.co.uk

Free postage and packing in the UK.

Other Michael O'Mara Humour titles include:

The Book of Urban Legends	ISBN 1-85479-932-0 pb £3.99
Born for the Job	ISBN 1-84317-099-X pb £5.99
The Complete Book of Farting	ISBN 1-85479-440-X pb £4.99
The Ultimate Insult	ISBN 1-85479-288-1 pb £5.99
Wicked Cockney Rhyming Slang	ISBN 1-85479-386-1 pb £3.99
The Wicked Wit of Jane Austen	ISBN 1-85479-652-6 hb £9.99
The Wicked Wit of Winston Churchill	ISBN 1-85479-529-5 hb £9.99
The Wicked Wit of Oscar Wilde	ISBN 1-85479-542-2 hb £9.99
The World's Stupidest Laws	ISBN 1-84317-172-4 pb £4.99
The World's Stupidest Signs	ISBN 1-84317-170-8 pb £4.99
More of the World's Stupidest Signs	ISBN 1-84317-032-9 pb £4.99
The World's Stupidest Last Words	ISBN 1-84317-021-3 pb £4.99
The World's Stupidest Inventions	ISBN 1-84317-036-1 pb £5.99
The World's Stupidest Criminals	ISBN 1-84317-171-6 pb £4.99
The World's Stupidest Instructions	ISBN 1-84317-078-7 pb £4.99
The World's Stupidest Sporting Screw-Ups	ISBN 1-84317-039-6 pb £4.99
The World's Stupidest Chat-Up Lines	ISBN 1-84317-019-1 pb £4.99
The World's Stupidest Husbands	ISBN 1-84317-168-6 pb £4.99
The World's Stupidest Celebrities	ISBN 1-84317-137-6 pb £4.99
The World's Stupidest Deaths	ISBN 1-84317-136-8 pb £4.99
Cricket: It's A Funny Old Game	ISBN 1-84317-090-6 pb £4.99
Football: It's A Funny Old Game	ISBN 1-84317-091-4 pb £4.99
Laughable Latin	ISBN 1-84317-097-3 pb £4.99
School Rules	ISBN 1-84317-100-7 pb £4.99
Sex Cheques (new edition)	ISBN 1-84317-121-X pb £3.50
The Timewaster Letters	ISBN 1-84317-108-2 pb £9.99
The Jordan Joke Book	ISBN 1-84317-120-1 pb £4.99
Speak Well English	ISBN 1-84317-088-4 pb £5.99
Shite's Unoriginal Miscellany	ISBN 1-84317-064-7 hb £9.99
Eats, Shites & Leaves	ISBN 1-84317-098-1 hb £9.99
A Shite History of Nearly Everything	ISBN 1-84317-138-4 hb £9.99